Inventory of Amphibians and Reptiles of Booker T. Washington National Monument

Technical Report NPS/NER/NRTR-2006/057

Joseph C. Mitchell, Ph. D.

Department of Biology
University of Richmond
Richmond, VA 23173

September 2006

U.S. Department of the Interior
National Park Service
Northeast Region
Philadelphia, Pennsylvania

The Northeast Region of the National Park Service (NPS) comprises national parks and related areas in 13 New England and Mid-Atlantic states. The diversity of parks and their resources are reflected in their designations as national parks, seashores, historic sites, recreation areas, military parks, memorials, and rivers and trails. Biological, physical, and social science research results, natural resource inventory and monitoring data, scientific literature reviews, bibliographies, and proceedings of technical workshops and conferences related to 38 of these park units in Maryland, New Jersey, Pennsylvania, Virginia, and West Virginia are disseminated through the NPS/NERCHAL Technical Report and Natural Resources Report series. The reports are a continuation of series with previous acronyms of NPS/PHSO and NPS/MAR, although they retain a consecutive numbering system. Individual parks may also disseminate information through their own report series.

Mention of trade names or commercial products does not constitute endorsement or recommendation for use by the National Park Service.

This technical report was produced by the University of Richmond under Cooperative Agreement 4560-B-0003, Supplemental Agreement No. 3, with the Northeast Region.

Reports in these series are produced in limited quantities and, as long as the supply lasts, may be obtained by sending a request to the address on the back cover. When original quantities are exhausted, copies may be requested from the NPS Technical Information Center (TIC), Denver Service Center, PO Box 25287, Denver, CO 80225-0287. A copy charge may be involved. To order from TIC, refer to document D-037.

This report may also be available as a downloadable portable document format file from the Internet at www.nps.gov/nero/science.

Please cite this publication as:

Mitchell, J. C. 2006. Inventory of Amphibians and Reptiles of Booker T. Washington National Monument. Technical Report NPS/NER/NRTR-2006/057. National Park Service, Northeast Region. Philadelphia, PA.

NPS D-037 September 2006

Table of Contents

Table of Contents (continued)

Figure

v

Tables

Appendixes

Executive Summary

This inventory was conducted at Booker T. Washington National Monument (BOWA), Virginia, in 2003 and 2004, to (1) document 90% of the amphibians (frogs, salamanders) and reptiles (turtles, lizards, snakes) of BOWA; 2) describe their associated habitats; and 3) provide park staff with conservation and management recommendations. Survey methods included visual encounter surveys, audio surveys, and road surveys, dipnets, minnow traps, and turtle traps.

Ten species of frogs, twelve salamander species, four turtle species, five lizard species, and 15 snake species were expected to occur at BOWA based on known distribution patterns in published literature. The proportion of species documented during this inventory was 50% for frogs, 33% for salamanders, 50% for turtles, 40% for lizards, and 33% for snakes. Total success for amphibians and reptiles was 41% and 38% of expected species, respectively. These success levels are below target levels; however, dry weather conditions in 2003 and the history of intense land use at BOWA likely contributed to the low species richness.

Seven habitat types used by amphibians and reptiles at BOWA were described from the field notes obtained during this inventory: grassland, mixed hardwoods and pine, mixed hardwoods, mixed pine, impoundment pond, floodplain pools, and streams. All habitats surveyed support multiple species and most species use both aquatic and terrestrial habitat types. Habitats that support relatively unique assemblages include mixed hardwood forests, impoundment pond, and floodplain pools. The combination of habitat types used by amphibians and reptiles at BOWA should be viewed as a matrix of habitats embedded within the landscape rather than as a series of separate habitat types. These habitats interact via movements of amphibians and reptiles and they should be protected and managed as a landscape complex.

Although this study documented less than 90% of the expected number of species for several groups, there are opportunities to register additional species. This can be accomplished in two ways by park staff: routine accumulation of digital photographs of road-kills or live amphibians and reptiles encountered with appropriate documentation appended to the digital image, and the use of natural history (animal) sighting cards filled out by knowledgeable visitors. Verification of new species records should be confirmed by a herpetologist.

Recommendations for BOWA resource management include: (1) Additional species inventory for frogs and snakes with further work to document snake species at BOWA including the use of coverboards as part of its sampling plan; (2) Areas of the park where there tend to be high concentrations of box turtles (*Terrapene carolina*), mixed hardwoods and stream floodplain, should be evaluated for adverse impacts before opening them to recreational activities; (3) The public should not be allowed to release any animals that have been in captivity, and park management should educate park visitors on this issue; (4) Specific habitats that should be monitored on a regular basis at BOWA for the occurrence and persistence of amphibians and reptiles include hardwood forests, small streams and their tributaries, and the small "farm" pond; (5) Educational materials should be developed on the ecology, flora and fauna, and their interactions with human history at BOWA; (6) Park raccoon (*Procyon lotor*) populations should be monitored, and population control measures implemented to protect all amphibians and reptiles, especially turtles and their nests; (7) Develop a comprehensive natural resource management plan to conserve amphibians and reptiles at BOWA; and (8) View long-term habitat management of amphibian and reptile habitats at BOWA within the context of the landscape matrix in and around the park.

Acknowledgments

Will Brown, Chris d'Orgeix, Todd Georgel, Elvira Lanham, and Lenny Leta assisted greatly in the field. I thank Resource Manager Timbo Simms for providing the collection permit, pertinent maps, some descriptive text of the park, and a variety of other forms of support for this project. I thank Beth Johnson, Sara Stevens, and John Karish, and the National Park Service for providing the funding for this project. Jim Comiskey provided information on the park and supported the completion of the report.

Introduction

Over the past decade, the National Park Service has been working to establish what is now called the Inventory and Monitoring Program (I&M Program). The principal and simplified functions of this program are to gather existing as well as new information about the natural resources in the parks and to make that information easily available at different levels to park resource managers, the scientific community, and the public. Although some of the national parks in the United States have conducted field research on their existing flora and fauna (e.g., Braswell 1988; Mitchell and Anderson 1994; Hobson 1997, 1998; Forester 2000; Tuberville et al. 2005), many parks have never completed baseline species inventories. Where information does exist it is often incomplete and inaccurate; and they sometimes include species well outside of their native range (Mitchell 2000b). For park managers to effectively maintain the biological diversity and ecological health of their parks, they must have a basic knowledge of what natural resources exist in parks, as well as an understanding of those factors that may threaten them. One of the first goals of the I&M Program has been to establish baseline biological inventories for vascular plant and vertebrate species in order to provide reliable species lists—a fundamental tool for management.

Beyond developing a documented species list, being able to associate species and their habitats within the parks is critical to planning and development of an effective land management strategy. Resource managers need credible information on species and habitat requirements to develop effective policies, guidelines, and management recommendations. Inventories that include locality, species richness, and population information will provide a valuable spatial database for managers to use for a variety of habitat-specific or site-specific management needs.

This report includes the results of a baseline amphibian and reptile inventory conducted at Booker T. Washington National Monument (BOWA) in 2002, 2003, and 2004. BOWA (119 ha [294 acres]) is located in the southwestern Virginia Piedmont, in Franklin County, 18 km (11 mi) northeast of the town of Rocky Mount. It functions as a demonstration farm for the late 1800s era, where several domestic species of livestock are maintained in pens and fields. All the fields are mowed occasionally, and the area around the visitors' center and farm buildings is maintained as a closely-cropped lawn. The entire park has hydrological links to the Atlantic Ocean via the Roanoke and Chowan river basins. Topography in this area is comprised of gently rolling hills, deeply weathered bedrock, and a few rock outcrops. The landscape varies from a stream floodplain and shallow ravines at about 250 m (820 ft) above mean sea level and terraces up to 305 m (1,000 ft) above mean sea level. Mixed pine and hardwood forests cover most of the park. Virginia pine (*Pinus virginiana*), loblolly (*Pinus taeda*), and table mountain pine (*Pinus pungens*) are the dominant coniferous species, while various oaks (*Quercus* spp.), hickory (*Carya* spp.), tulip poplar (*Liriodendron tulipifera*), and other hardwoods occur in terrestrial areas, and red maples (*Acer rubrum*) and black willow (*Salix nigra*) occupy the wetter areas. The park is approximately 80% wooded and 20% open field. Gill's Creek is the primary stream with three tributaries, including Jack-O-Lantern Branch which drains the working demonstration farm portion of the park.

The biological resources of BOWA include a variety of animals and plants characteristic of a mix of southwestern Virginia Piedmont and Central Appalachian mixed deciduous forest species.

At least 193 species of trees, shrubs, and herbaceous plants occur in the park (National Park Service documentation, Timbo Simms, Natural Resource Manager, pers. comm.). The composition of the fauna is unknown. For more information, see the park's Web site at www.nps.gov/BOWA/nature/.

A search of the literature and museum specimen records for Booker T. Washington National Monument confirmed the lack of information on amphibian and reptile species occurrence in the park. No museum records were found in the Smithsonian Institution (NMNH) or other museums. There is no published literature on the amphibians and reptiles of BOWA. Based on known distributions (Mitchell 1994; Conant and Collins 1998; Mitchell and Reay 1999), 22 amphibian species and 24 reptile species could potentially occur at BOWA (Appendix A).

The BOWA herp inventory was conducted on May 9, 2002 (on an initial visit), from March 20 to September 27, 2003, and on May 29, 2004 (Appendix B). The project objectives were to: 1) document 90% of the amphibians and reptiles at BOWA; 2) describe their associated habitats; and 3) provide park staff with conservation and management recommendations.

The inventory of amphibians and reptiles at BOWA was conducted at all accessible portions of the Park. Booker T. Washington National Monument consists of one main geographic unit.

Eight habitat types were described by field crews as being used by amphibians and reptiles in BOWA[1]. Common and scientific names of the flora follow Radford et al. (1968). The habitat and microhabitat (location where animal was first sighted, e.g., under log, along pool margin, moving in open) was noted for each capture and observation.

Grasslands (GRA) - Open fields dominated by grasses that are mowed on a regular to irregular basis or other land uses that have removed the forest canopy and created small to large patches of grass habitat. These areas include mixed grasses (Bermuda grass [*Cynodon dactylon*], velvet grass [*Holcus lanatus*], sweet vernal grass [*Anthoxanthum odoratum*], and broomsedge [*Andropogon virginicus*]) and herbs (dog fennel [*Anthemis* sp.], St. John's wort [*Hypericum* sp.], wood sorrel [*Oxalis* sp.], and dandelion [*Taraxacum officinale*]).

Mixed hardwoods and pine (MHP) - Common wooded habitat at BOWA, consisting of loblolly pine, Virginia pine, and hardwoods. Dominant trees include sweet gum, various oaks, and tulip poplar. Understory trees include American holly (*Ilex opaca*), dogwood (*Cornus florida*), some red maple, and ironwood (*Carpinus caroliniana*). Vines include trumpet vine (*Campsis radicans*) and greenbrier (*Smilax rotundifolia*), with an herbaceous layer of Pennsylvania smartweed (*Persicaria pennsylvanica*) and grasses (*Panicum* sp.). Downed-woody debris varies throughout this habitat type. Many areas have a thin layer of leaf litter with exposed, bare ground in some places.

Mixed hardwoods (MHW) - hardwood forests at BOWA lack a clear dominant overstory species, and include oaks (*Quercus* alba, *Q. falcata*, *Q. velutina*), hickory, tulip poplar, red maple, beech (*Fagus grandifolia*), and blackgum (*Nyssa sylvatica*). The understory consists primarily of American holly, dogwood, blueberries (*Vaccinium* sp.) and huckleberries (*Gaylussacia* spp.), and saplings of overstory trees. The herbaceous layer is generally sparse, consisting of partridge berry (*Mitchella repens*), Pennsylvania smartweed, grasses, and seedlings of hardwoods, and occasionally loblolly pine. Downed woody debris is a common feature on the forest floor on a thin to moderate layer of decomposing leaves.

Mixed pine (MPI) - Loblolly pine is the most common species at BOWA, but some areas are largely comprised of Virginia pine. In some areas, hardwood trees (*A. rubrum*, *L. stryaciflua*) are scattered among the pines, usually as understory trees. Herbs are sparse and include Pennsylvania smartweed and partridge berry and vines include poison ivy (*Toxicodendron radicans*) and greenbrier. Downed woody debris is less common than in the hardwood sites.

Impoundments (IMP) - The primary impoundment at BOWA is a small, shallow pond in the demonstration farm area. This pond is surrounded by maintained field and lawn with a few large hardwood trees nearby. It is generally considered and functions as a farm pond.

---

[1] It is recommended that sampling location coordinates be cross-referenced with future vegetation maps to standardize habitat type nomenclature.

Farm Buildings (FB) - Several farm buildings in the demonstration area are relatively old and offer habitats for several species of amphibians and reptiles. These structures were searched visually and non-destructively.

Floodplain Pools (FDPL) - Very few ephemeral pools (natural depressions in the landscape that hold water for varying times during the year, usually winter to summer) occur in the floodplain of Gill's Creek. The better ones are just outside the park property. Flood events probably help to maintain these pools on a periodic basis.

Stream (STR) - Gill's Creek bisects the southern portion of the park. This is a relatively narrow, shallow, sandy river, with several deep pools and undercut banks. The substrate is largely bedrock and some areas have patches of small rocks bordering the stream. Tree and shrub vegetation overhang the river in some places. There are few debris dams on the river within BOWA. Several springs are associated with Jack-O-Lantern Branch (the primary one in the demonstration farm area) and other tributaries.

Methods

Expected Species List Development

A list of species expected to occur at BOWA was developed based on Mitchell (1994), Conant and Collins (1998), and Mitchell and Reay (1999). The final expected species list is composed of 22 species of amphibians and 24 species of reptiles (Appendix A).

Sampling

After an initial site visit on May 9, 2002, actual field survey work was conducted during amphibian and reptile activity seasons (late winter to September) in 2003 and 2004. The field schedule is outlined in detail in Appendix B.

We used a variety of sampling techniques to conduct the inventory at BOWA. These sampling techniques are described in more detail for amphibians by Heyer et al. (1994) and Mitchell (2000a), and for reptiles by Jones (1986), Mitchell (1994), and Blomberg and Shine (1996). The protocols may vary when applied to monitoring (Heyer et al. 1994).

Audio Survey

Audio surveys, the detection of a frog species by its species-specific vocalization, were conducted during the day and also by night by listening for frog vocalizations at known wetland sites. Audio surveys conducted as part of this inventory were not time-constrained.

Dipnet Survey

Dipnet surveys are amphibian species detection through sampling with dipnets in aquatic microhabitats. The dipnets used in this inventory were D-ring aquatic nets with a fine mesh bag (Wards Biological Supply Co., Rochester, NY). This technique captured adults and larvae.

Visual Encounter Survey (VES)

Visual encounter surveys are unstructured searches of selected habitats and microhabitats conducted by an experienced field herpetologist when the probability of encounter is high (appropriate weather and season for the targeted species). Visual encounter surveys are sometimes referred to as haphazard or random searching. Random searches, however, are seldom random, as an experienced herpetologist will preferentially search microhabitats that may yield results. Visual encounter surveys were conducted by walking in an unstructured manner through a selected habitat type, observing active amphibians and reptiles, as well as turning logs and other surface objects to uncover animals. Binoculars are used for searching water surfaces, logs, margins of wetlands, and basking places for frogs, lizards, snakes, and turtles. Visual encounter surveys conducted as part of this inventory were not time-constrained.

Minnow Traps and Turtle Traps

Minnow traps and turtle traps were not used in the survey of BOWA.

Animal Measurements

All captured animals were handled in accordance with National guidelines developed by the professional herpetological societies. No animals were harmed in the process, each being released at the site of capture.

All amphibians and reptiles captured were identified to species. Common and scientific names for amphibians and reptiles follow Crother (2000). Most animals were measured and weighed and gender determined. All measurements were recorded in millimeters and weights were recorded in grams. Body and tail measurements of amphibians were taken using plastic rulers, metric tapes, and calipers. Weights were taken with Pesola® scales and Ohaus Scout electronic field balances (Forestry Suppliers, Inc.). Animals seen or heard in the field but not captured were included in the database simply as observations (= present).

Frogs

Snout-Vent Length (SVL) was measured for frogs from the tip of the snout to the cloacal opening while the body was maintained in a straight line (i.e., making sure the sacral hump was flat).

Salamanders

For salamanders the SVL was taken from the tip of the snout to the posterior margin of the vent. Tail length was measured from the posterior vent margin to the tip of the tail when the tail was original and complete (not broken). For tails that were broken or had regenerated portions, the original tail portion was measured plus the length of the regenerated portion (resulting in numbers such as 19+21).

Lizards

Straight-line SVL was taken from the tip of the snout to the posterior margin of the vent (anal plate) for all lizards captured. Tail length was taken from the posterior margin of the anal plate to the tip of the tail when the tail was original and complete (not broken). When tails were broken or had regenerated portions, then the original tail was measured plus the length of the regenerated portion (resulting in numbers such as 32+26).

Snakes

For snakes the SVL was taken from the tip of the snout to the posterior margin of the anal plate with a metric tape, following the body curves. Tail length was taken from the posterior margin of the anal plate to the tip of the tail. Broken tails were simply noted, as these animals do not regenerate their tails like amphibians and many lizards. Snakes were weighed in cloth or plastic bags, subtracting the weight of the bag to obtain the snake's weight.

Turtles

For turtles carapace length (CL) and plastron lengths (PL) were taken with calipers (dial and tree) as straight-line measurements from the anterior-most point to the posterior-most point on the shell. The bar on the calipers was always parallel to the turtle's vertebral column.

Locational Data

Location data for Booker T. Washington National Monument was collected using Magellan 310 and 315 hand-held GPS units. Location information was recorded where an individual animal was caught or observed. When a defined terrestrial habitat area was searched, such as a field, a coordinate was taken at the center[2]. For wetlands, (e.g., pond, seasonal ponds) coordinates were taken where minnow traps were set, resulting in a single coordinate at one point along the margin. Search area boundaries changed once a new habitat type was encountered.

Photo Vouchers

Photographs were taken of at least the first individual of each species captured using a Nikon 6006 SLR with macro lens and Fuji chrome Provia 100F slide film; slides were scanned at 300 dpi with an HP Scan jet 5370C slide scanner. Digital pictures were taken using a Nikon Coolpix 775 digital camera set at 1600x1200 pixels (Normal). A list of photo vouchers by number and species name is provided in Appendix C.

---

[2] Whether terrestrial or aquatic amphibians and reptiles may move considerable distances through the habitat during daily or seasonal activities. Thus, single coordinates for areas locations was deemed appropriate, as long as the habitat was uniform.

Results

Inventory Results

Ten species of frogs, 12 species of salamanders, four species of turtles, five species of lizards, and 15 species of snakes were expected to occur in BOWA based on available habitat types and known species distribution patterns (Mitchell 1994; Conant and Collins 1998; Mitchell and Reay 1999) (Table 1; Appendix A). The current inventory documented nine species of amphibians and nine species of reptiles; these included five frog species (50% of the frog species expected to occur in the park), four salamander species (33% of the expected salamander species), two turtle species (50% of the turtle species expected to occur in the park), two lizard species (40% of the lizard species expected to occur), and five snake species (33% of the snake species expected to occur in the park). A map of the locations where all amphibians and reptiles were inventoried is shown in Figure 1. Total capture success was 41% for amphibians and 38% for reptiles.

A total of 137 individual animals were captured or observed during this inventory, including 32 amphibians (22 frogs, 10 salamanders) and 105 reptiles (10 turtles, 77 lizards, 18 snakes). Totals include all individual adults, frog tadpoles, and salamander larvae captured or observed. Pond-breeding frogs (*Rana clamitans*) and terrestrial toads (*Bufo americanus*) dominated the frog fauna numerically, but none was observed more than six times. Two species of ambystomatid salamanders dominated this faunal group numerically, marbled salamander (*Ambystoma opacum*) and mole salamander (*A. talpoideum*) [according to the table, neither was observed in the park]. Only the one stream-breeding species, northern spring salamander (*Gyrinophilus porphyriticus*) was captured in any numbers (five). Neither species of terrestrial salamanders (*Plethodon cinereus*, *P. cylindraceus*) was encountered in BOWA.

Eastern box turtles were the most numerous chelonian species found at BOWA. Individuals of only one freshwater species were found, the snapping turtle (*Chelydra serpentina*). Two lizards were found, both apparently abundant on BOWA, the five-lined skink (*Eumeces fasciatus*) and the eastern fence lizard (*Sceloporus undulatus*). The latter was found in relatively large numbers. The snake fauna was the most difficult to sample. In BOWA, the eastern ratsnake (*Elaphe obsoleta*) was the most numerous species seen in the hardwood forests in the park and in the out buildings. One species of snake, the northern watersnake (*Nerodia sipedon*), was found in association with Gill's Creek and its tributaries.

No species listed as state or federally threatened were found during this inventory. Although no venomous snakes were found during this survey, the probability of the northern copperhead (*Agkistrodon contortrix*) occurring on BOWA is probably high.

Sampling Success

Table 2 provides the number of individuals of each species documented at BOWA in relation to the sampling methods used. More species were detected using the visual encounter survey protocol than any other protocol (16 of the 19 species encountered in 2003 and 2004). Frog vocalizations resulted in one species not encountered using VES (northern spring peeper [*Pseudacris crucifer*]). One salamander species was revealed by dipnet sampling and three by the VES method. All turtle, lizard, and snake species were found during VES surveys.

Table 1. Checklist of amphibians and reptiles of Booker T. Washington National Monument, Virginia. Expected column equals species that should occur in BOWA given distribution patterns (Mitchell and Reay 1999) and available habitat. Confirmed equals number of individuals observed or captured during the 2003–2004 inventory. Observations of species without capture to voucher with a photograph are noted as "obs" representing Observed.

Scientific name	Common name	Expected	Confirmed
Frogs			
Acris crepitans	northern cricket frog	X	
Bufo americanus	American toad	X	X
Bufo fowleri	Fowler's toad	X	
Hyla chrysoscelis	Cope's gray treefrog	X	X
Hyla versicolor	eastern gray treefrog	X	
Pseudacris crucifer	northern spring peeper	X	X
Pseudacris feriarum	upland chorus frog	X	
Rana catesbeiana	American bullfrog	X	X
Rana clamitans	northern green frog	X	X
Rana palustris	pickerel frog	X	
Salamanders			
Ambystoma maculatum	spotted salamander	X	
Ambystoma opacum	marbled salamander	X	
Desmognathus fuscus	dusky salamander	X	X
Desmognathus monticola	seal salamander	X	
Eurycea cirrigera	southern two-lined salamander	X	X
Eurycea guttolineata	three-lined salamander	X	
Gyrinophilus porphyriticus	spring salamander	X	X
Hemidactylium scutatum	four-toed salamander	X	
Notophthalmus viridescens	red-spotted newt	X	
Plethodon cylindraceus	white-spotted slimy salamander	X	
Plethodon cinereus	red-backed salamander	X	
Pseudotriton ruber	northern red salamander	X	X
Turtles			
Chelydra serpentina	common snapping turtle	X	X
Chrysemys picta	eastern painted turtle	X	
Sternotherus odoratus	stinkpot	X	
Terrapene carolina	eastern box turtle	X	X
Lizards			
Cnemidophorus sexlineatus	six-lined racerunner	X	
Eumeces fasciatus	five-lined skink	X	X
Eumeces laticeps	broad-headed skink	X	
Sceloporus undulatus	eastern fence lizard	X	X
Scincella lateralis	ground skink	X	
Snakes			
Agkistrodon contortrix	northern copperhead	X	
Carphophis amoenus	eastern worm snake	X	X
Coluber constrictor	northern black racer	X	
Diadophis punctatus	northern ring-necked snake	X	X
Elaphe obsoleta	eastern ratsnake	X	X
Heterodon platirhinos	eastern hog-nosed snake	X	
Lampropeltis calligaster	mole kingsnake	X	
Lampropeltis getula	eastern kingsnake	X	
Nerodia sipedon	northern watersnake	X	X

Table 1. Checklist of amphibians and reptiles of Booker T. Washington National Monument, Virginia. Expected column equals species that should occur in BOWA given distribution patterns (Mitchell and Reay 1999) and available habitat. Confirmed equals number of individuals observed or captured during the 2003–2004 inventory. Observations of species without capture to voucher with a photograph are noted as "obs" representing Observed (continued).

Scientific name	Common name	Expected	Confirmed
Snakes (continued)			
Opheodrys aestivus	rough greensnake	X	
Regina septemvittata	queen snake	X	
Storeria dekayi	northern brownsnake	X	
Storeria occipitomaculata	red-bellied snake	X	X
Thamnophis sauritus	northern ribbonsnake	X	
Thamnophis sirtalis	eastern gartersnake	X	

Figure 1. Map showing observation and capture locations for amphibians and reptiles in Booker T. Washington National Monument.

Table 2. Number of individuals of each herpetological species documented by sampling method at Booker T. Washington National Monument during 2003 and 2004 inventories. Numbers in parentheses are observations of individual amphibians and reptiles provided by Timbo Simms, BOWA Natural Resource Manager.

Scientific name	Audio	Dipnet	VES
Frogs			
Bufo americanus	1		5 (1)
Hyla chrysoscelis	3		2
Pseudacris crucifer	3		
Rana catesbeiana			2
Rana clamitans			6
Salamanders			
Desmognathus fuscus			3
Eurycea cirrigera			1
Gyrinophilus porphyriticus		5	
Pseudotriton ruber			1
Turtles			
Chelydra serpentina			2 (2)
Terrapene carolina			8
Lizards			
Eumeces fasciatus			15
Sceloporus undulatus			62
Snakes			
Carphophis amoenus			2
Diadophis punctatus			1
Elaphe obsoleta			8
Nerodia sipedon			5
Storeria occipitomaculata			2
Total	7	5	125 (3)

Species/Habitat Associations

Distribution of capture and observation records for amphibians and reptiles among eight habitat types revealed that no species is a habitat specialist at BOWA (Table 3). However, three habitat types in this park support a high diversity of amphibians and reptiles. These are mixed hardwoods, mixed hardwood and pine, and streams. The mixed hardwood forests support a wide diversity of amphibians and reptiles with relatively large numbers. Mixed hardwoods and pine supported relatively high species richness but few individuals. Pine stands support very few amphibians and reptiles. The open grasslands with the wooden fences supported a large population of eastern fence lizards, several five-lined skinks, a few eastern ratsnakes, and one individual each of the green frog (*Rana clamitans*) and box turtle.

Amphibian species with five or more records confined to a single habitat type include the American toad (*Bufo americanus*) and the northern spring salamander (Table 3). Reptile species with five or more occurrences in a single habitat type include the eastern box turtle, five-lined skink, eastern fence lizard, and eastern ratsnake.

Table 3. Numbers of individual amphibians and reptiles captured or observed among eight habitat types at Booker T. Washington National Monument, during 2003 and 2004. Abbreviations as in the text.

Scientific name	GRA	MHP	MHW	MPI	FB	IMP	FDPL	STR
Frogs								
Bufo americanus		1	5				1	
Hyla chrysoscelis		2	4					
Pseudacris crucifer			2				1	
Rana catesbeiana						2		
Rana clamitans	1							4
Salamanders								
Desmognathus fuscus								3
Eurycea cirrigera								1
Gyrinophilus porphyriticus								5
Pseudotriton ruber			1					
Turtles								
Chelydra serpentina								2
Terrapene carolina	1	1	6					
Lizards								
Eumeces fasciatus	6	1	7		1			
Sceloporus undulatus	52	1	8	1				
Snakes								
Carphophis amoenus		1	1					
Diadophis punctatus		1						
Elaphe obsoleta	6				2			
Nerodia sipedon						2		2
Storeria occipitomaculata			2					
Total	66	8	36	1	3	4	2	17

[1] Habitat types include: Grasslands (GRA), Mixed hardwoods and pine (MHP), Mixed hardwoods (MHW), Mixed pine (MPI), Farm buildings (FB), Impoundments (IMP), Floodplain Pools (FDPL), and Stream (STR)

Discussion

Inventory

Amphibians and reptiles are highly seasonal animals whose activity patterns respond to changes in climate, temperature, and precipitation. Thus, a complete inventory of amphibians and reptiles can be a challenge during short-term surveys. Rainfall in 2003 was generally normal to above normal except in January when precipitation total was nearly 3.8 cm (1.5 in) below normal (average departure from normal during February–December was 5 cm [2.0 in]; January departure was -3.5 cm [-1.39 in]; Huddleston weather station [Rocky Mount station had missing data for many months], NOAA Climate Data Center, Asheville, NC). In 2004, precipitation was below normal for January through May (average departure was -3.12 cm [-1.23 in]), but above normal for the rest of the year (average departure was 3.3 cm [1.31 in]). These variable precipitation patterns had some affect on encounter rates with some of the amphibians and many of the reptiles. Most snakes, in particular, are very secretive and active only when surface conditions are especially suited. Thus, some of the species likely to be present in BOWA were missed in this inventory due to our not being present when the weather conditions were suitable for these difficult-to-find species.

Notwithstanding the climatic limitations, the species encountered during this survey represent a moderately robust list for all groups of amphibians and reptiles at BOWA, except snakes. Most of the frog species were found during both years of inventories. The success for salamanders (33%) is a result of their occurrence in small streams, tributaries, and freshwater springs in BOWA. We found no fully terrestrial species (typically red-backed salamander [*Plethodon cinereus*] and white-spotted slimy salamander [*P. cylindraceus*] in this area). This suggests that the hardwood forests have not reached maturity enough to provide the leaf litter and soil depth to allow these hardwood forest species to occur there. This situation is also likely a function of the history of the heavy use of the landscape in this area. The percentage for lizards was only 40% with two of the five expected species encountered at BOWA. One species (*Eumeces laticeps*) may not occur in the park due to historical land use (they require mature trees). The other species not encountered (Table 1) may be due to the extreme dry conditions or distribution patchiness. The two turtle species we encountered are commonly found in forested landscapes and slow-moving streams and rivers in this region.

Only five of the 15 species of snakes expected to occur at BOWA were documented during the 2003-2004 inventory. Snake species that were not encountered, but were expected to occur at BOWA include the northern copperhead, northern black racer (*Coluber constrictor*), eastern hog-nosed snake (*Heterodon platirhinos*), mole kingsnake (*Lampropeltis calligaster*), eastern kingsnake (*Lampropeltis getula*), rough greensnake (*Opheodrys* aestivus), northern brownsnake (*Storeria dekayi*), eastern ribbonsnake (*Thamnophis sauritus*), and eastern gartersnake (*Thamnophis sirtalis*). Additional field trips and chance observations in favorable weather conditions would be required to add more snake species to the park's list. Many snakes are active for only short periods of time during favorable weather, usually warm and wet periods (Wright and Wright 1957; Gibbons and Semlitsch 1987), and few species of snakes move with sufficient frequency to be encountered when it is dry. Snakes, in general, can be especially difficult to survey; many are secretive and occur in limited numbers (Gibbons et al. 1997).

Leiden et al. (1999) demonstrated with multiple techniques that 66% of the total snake species expected were caught in the first 75 days of sampling, but that an additional 325 days of sampling would be required to collect 90% of the total number expected. Whiteman et al. (1995) and Gibbons et al. (1997) showed that it took over 22 years to discover one snake species on the Savannah River site, an area that has been intensively studied for over 40 years.

Based on distribution patterns of amphibian and reptile species in Virginia (Mitchell 1994; Conant and Collins 1998; Mitchell and Reay 1999), all of the species encountered during this survey were expected to occur in BOWA.

Sampling Method Efficiency

Because amphibians and reptiles are notoriously secretive animals, successful species documentation depends upon the use of multiple capture techniques in both wetland and terrestrial habitats (Corn and Bury 1990; Heyer et al. 1994; Ryan et al. 2002). Determining which method(s) are most effective depends on the goal of the inventory, as well as the behaviors and habitats of target species expected to be encountered. Visual encounter surveys often detect the greatest numbers of species, as was the case in this survey, detecting 16 of the 18 species encountered (Table 2). It is important to keep in mind though, when choosing to use VES, that this survey method will not provide quantitative data useful for estimating population size or structure, primary habitat preferences, or habitat use during different life stages or distribution. It is also important to note that visual encounter surveys are difficult to replicate in future efforts, as they lack rigor from a sampling and statistical perspective, and are essentially qualitative rather than quantitative. Their primary usefulness is in assessing species richness of the study area.

The results of this survey also indicate that methods vary in their effectiveness at detecting different species, even those within the same taxonomic group such as frogs. Considering the diversity of amphibians and reptiles and the variability in their size, modes of reproduction, patterns of habitat use, degree of habitat specialization, and life history, this is expected. To account for this, a generalized, multi-habitat inventory should always incorporate a number of different methods. Choice of methods will depend to a certain extent on the relative importance placed on detecting species presence versus generating quantitative estimates of abundance, population size and structure, and habitat comparisons, as well as what the potential species are. Based on the BOWA inventory, audio surveys and dipnet surveys, when augmented by visual encounter surveys, were most effective for the generalized inventory of this park.

For frogs, the combination of audio, dipnet, and visual encounter surveys proved to be the most effective documentation methods for inventory. Use of minnow traps may be an effective way to inventory salamander larvae and frog tadpoles in shallow lotic habitats, but such places were uncommon at BOWA. These traps should always be considered when developing additional inventory plans. Other survey methods such as road surveys can be an effective technique for documenting snakes, turtles, and frogs, although success depends greatly on weather, seasonal activity patterns, and the availability of roads. The road survey method proved unreliable in BOWA.

One method that should be considered specifically for the documentation of snakes is coverboard surveys. Coverboards, quarter sheets of plywood, roofing tin, or other similar material, laid out in selected areas on the ground could have been used to potentially enhance snake capture success at BOWA. Coverboards were not used in this study, as it was assumed that there would be sufficient logs and other surface cover objects available throughout the park for searching. Unfortunately there were fewer natural cover objects available than expected in areas that might have harbored small snakes. Other methods that could potentially be used to survey snakes include glueboards, but these can result in the death of animals so are not highly recommended, or drift fences with pitfall traps. Drift fence and pitfall traps require a large effort to install and operate (Gibbons and Semlitsch 1981). In the future, additional work to document the snake fauna at BOWA should include the use of coverboards placed in selected habitats around the park.

Species-Habitat Associations

Protection of selected habitats could allow viable populations of native amphibians and reptiles to persist in BOWA. Amphibians and reptiles function in a landscape context (Semlitsch 2003), and a mix of habitat types is essential for their existence in the park. Long-term preservation of the amphibian and reptile populations at BOWA will require the management and maintenance of a variety of habitat types. Factors that may impact this mosaic should be identified and addressed in the park management plan. Habitats that support relatively unique assemblages of these vertebrates include hardwood forests, the riparian zone of Gill's Creek and its floodplain pools, and the wetlands (pond and spring) in the demonstration farm area at BOWA.

The habitat classification used in the current study was based on general field descriptions and is indicative of the ecological conditions favorable to the amphibians and reptiles (e.g., Wright and Wright 1957; Martof et al. 1980; Mitchell 1994; Conant and Collins 1998) that we found in BOWA. These animals rely more on the environmental structure (shelter, temperature, relative humidity) provided by plant community environments rather than individual plant species composition (pers. obs.). Most amphibians and reptiles use multiple habitat types that are adjacent to one another during daily and seasonal movements (e.g., Reinert 1993; Buhlmann 2001; Semlitsch 2003), and may travel one or more kilometers (e.g., Gregory et al. 1987; Semlitsch 1998; Semlitsch and Bodie 1998; Pauley et al. 2000). Some habitats may be used by species only during movements from one primary habitat to another and other species can move among several habitat types in a single day or season. It is important to remember that a record in a single habitat type may only be a snapshot of habitat preference by a species. Only detailed studies of movements using radio-telemetry can reveal all the habitats used by a species in a given area (e.g., Reinert 1993; Carter et al. 1999).

Important components of the existing BOWA landscape necessary for maintaining amphibian and reptile species includes a matrix or combination of freshwater seasonal streams, springs, and hardwood forest habitats throughout the park. Loss of one of these habitat types will result in the loss of these species in the park. Appropriate corridors connecting hardwood forest patches are essential landscape features that greatly influence the viability of amphibian and reptile populations in BOWA.

Another important factor to consider in the conservation of amphibian and reptile species is their movement between foraging, overwintering, and breeding areas. Maintaining viable populations of these animals in the park will require that they be able to disperse across habitats and among breeding areas. Design of dispersal corridors should be included in any species management plan. As recently discussed in the literature, habitat conservation strategies for amphibians and reptiles must include the maintenance and preservation of a core habitat composed of breeding sites and the terrestrial habitat surrounding them (165 m [540 ft] average) surrounded by an additional buffer zone beyond that (Semlitsch and Jensen 2001).

Aquatic habitats (small impoundment, floodplain pools) support a diverse array of species, with many species using more than one of these habitats in BOWA. Treefrogs and ranid frogs were the dominant fauna found in the park's primary farm impoundment and springs, while several streamside salamanders and freshwater turtles were found primarily in stream habitats.

Although habitat type was collected as part of the inventory conducted at BOWA, this information can only provide a simple snapshot of habitat types that amphibian and reptile species use in this park. It is important for the park to remember that it would be incorrect to say that most of the species were captured or documented in Mixed-Hardwood habitat (MHW) as shown in Table 3, without considering the number and extent of the embedded springs within those habitats. MHP and MHW habitats without springs would most likely support a completely different assemblage of amphibian and reptile species than what was recorded during this inventory. Again, it must be stressed, when considering management of areas that support herpetological species within the park, a complete picture of the existing landscape matrix must be included. The habitat information collected as part of this inventory can only provide a general picture of where specific amphibian and reptile species might be found in the park, and no quantitative analysis can be done to rank the use of habitat types by species.

Management Issues

Effective amphibian and reptile management first requires identification of threats. The threats to these vertebrates on BOWA include mortality from vehicular traffic, human disturbance or killing, subsidized predators, and habitat loss or alteration. Removal of animals by humans for personal pets or the commercial pet trade constitutes an unknown threat level, as there is no data to evaluate this impact. Habitat loss is not considered a major threat at BOWA. Future plans for alteration of areas of park land that may include habitat loss should be reviewed thoroughly and losses prevented when possible. Specific areas to which to pay special attention include the farm impoundment, the springs, Gill's Creek and its tributaries, and the full-canopy hardwood forests. These habitats should be maintained as natural areas with amphibians and reptiles in mind.

Conclusions and Management Recommendations

Habitat Restricted Species

Most of the herpetofaunal species found at BOWA are those that occur throughout the Virginia Piedmont. Many of these species use a variety of habitats during daily movements, as well as seasonal movements to breeding pools and ponds. Most species can be considered as habitat generalists except for the stream salamanders and the pool-breeding ambystomatid salamanders. Additional inventory work on each individual habitat type should be considered to better understand the abundance and distributions of amphibians and reptiles within them.

Amphibians and Reptiles as Indicators of Ecosystem Health

During a recent study on box turtles it was found that nearly all turtles captured in parts of Virginia had high levels of organochlorine pesticide in their systems. Because box turtles are so long-lived they can accumulate chemicals from the environment. A good example is the development of aural (ear) abscesses as a result of vitamin A deficiency caused by organochlorine pesticide contamination (Holladay et al. 2001; Brown et al. 2004). Because of these recent studies on box turtles it is becoming more and more apparent that they may be excellent indicators of ecosystem condition and health. During this inventory at BOWA no turtles with aural abscesses were found, suggesting that this may not currently be a problem at BOWA. Environmental contamination by pollutants from increased human development of the area around BOWA may produce such problems that could be additionally monitored by annual surveys of box turtle population conditions at the park.

Ecotoxicology studies of herbicide and pesticide effects on amphibians have not been thorough and often use only a laboratory species not found in North America (McDiarmid and Mitchell 2000). Spraying herbicides and pesticides in and over terrestrial and wetland habitats could produce harmful results to amphibian populations, especially at the larval stage. The use of larvacides for mosquito control (West Nile virus) in wetlands such as seasonal ponds is also likely to be harmful to larval-staged amphibians. Decisions to use chemicals for natural resource management should thus be made with extreme caution, and larval populations monitored both prior to and post spraying of pesticides. Nearly all commercial pesticides and herbicides are now considered harmful to amphibian larvae and adults (Relyea and Mills 2001; Relyea 2004, 2005). Broadcast applications of commercial chemicals in BOWA should be evaluated fully with all impacts in mind before being allowed to be used.

Education

Educational materials should be developed on the ecology, flora, and fauna, and their interactions with human history at BOWA. Such materials will properly advise visitors of the value of this park to natural resources, and instruct them on the context within which the historical actions took place.

Additional Inventory Work

Additional species documentation work would be of value for all species of amphibians and reptiles in BOWA. Such documentation provided by park staff and visitor observations could add several species to the known list. Further work to document snake species at BOWA should include the use of coverboards as part of its sampling plan. Additional documentation to add to the overall amphibian and reptile species list for BOWA could be accomplished in three ways: (1) routine accumulation of digital photographs of road-kills, especially snakes, with appropriate documentation (date and location); (2) use of several coverboard arrays monitored periodically; and (3) use of natural history (animal) sighting cards filled out by knowledgeable visitors. Initiation of the latter program would result in a valuable source of information for natural resource management staff if accompanied by verifiable information such as a photograph or specimen. In addition, further herpetological work at BOWA could include methods for acquiring species abundance and detailed distribution information for all species documented during this inventory.

The copperhead, the only venomous snake in the area, is not a common snake at BOWA, and was not found during our survey. Their low occurrence frequency and apparent spotty distribution in the area suggests that education may be the only reasonable approach that could be used by park personnel to address their presence and their potential threat to humans. Park personnel should be trained on field emergency treatment of copperhead snakebite, realizing that such bites are not fatal.

Habitat Management

Long-term habitat management at BOWA would benefit if management issues and potential construction impacts were viewed within the context of the park's landscape matrix as a whole. Any change to mixed hardwood forests, the ephemeral pond, and river floodplain at BOWA, for example, may have consequences to the streamside salamander complex and the box turtle population. Many individuals of the latter species are long-lived (30–100 years old, Dodd 2001).

Mowing is a weekly, if not daily, activity in BOWA. Such operations are well known for killing box turtles. Thus, blade height on mowers should be set at least six inches high or higher to avoid killing box turtles that may be walking across lawns.

Specific habitats should be monitored at BOWA for the occurrence and persistence of amphibians and reptiles, including the farm pond, springs, and mature hardwoods. Hardwood forest habitats are critical areas for some amphibians and reptiles. Forests with full to partial canopy and a well-defined forest floor with downed woody debris and leaves provide important microhabitat for several species and should be maintained with the concept of "old growth" in mind.

The impoundment should be maintained as a small breeding pond for amphibians. Fish should not be stocked in this pond. If any fish are present they should be removed; this may take an effort to draw down the pond or wait for a serious drought to help the process. Adjacent emergent vegetation and cattails (*Typha* sp.) should be encouraged and maintained as refugia for frogs. Do not clear the hardwood forest adjacent to this pond.

Gill's Creek and its riparian floodplain should be maintained in as natural a state as possible. Land clearing and other activities should be evaluated as to their effects on these sensitive habitats before such activities take place. Such activities should be avoided if at all possible.

A comprehensive natural habitat management plan for the conservation of native species and their habitats should be developed for BOWA. Its natural history has received little to no attention. A management plan for this historic site would ensure that this area is maintained in sufficient natural conditions to allow the persistence of the native amphibian and reptile fauna. The working/research committee for such a plan could include experts in all floral and faunal groups, as well as forest and wetland conservation biologists.

Vehicles and Recreational Activities

Garber and Burger (1995) found that opening an area to recreation resulted in the complete loss of a wood turtle (*Clemmys insculpta*) population, caused primarily by removal of turtles by humans and dogs. Humans pick up box turtles and will remove them or at least carry them to other locations in the park. Removal of even one mature adult female results in the loss of a critically important reproductive individual to the population. Populations of such long-lived species depend entirely on their mature adults to remain stable or increase. Their removal will result in population decline and extirpation. Areas of the park where there tend to be high concentrations of box turtles, such as the river floodplain and mature hardwood forests, should be evaluated before opening them to recreational activities.

Rates of mortality on roads adjacent to the park are unknown, but could be significant for some species. Knowing these rates and better understanding the seasonality of road mortalities in the park will help resource managers to better manage potential problem areas and allow steps to be taken to minimize vehicular mortality on park roads. If there are areas where animal mortality is commonplace, then evaluation of the potential for ecopassages may be warranted.

Exotics and Subsidized Predators

Scavenging/predatory mammals usually exist at higher population densities in areas of high human use due to garbage and discarded food and structures as shelters. Raccoons, which are notorious for killing and eating turtle adults and eggs in nests, can dramatically decrease populations of these species. They also eat frogs and any other amphibian or reptile they can catch. Animals that qualify as subsidized predators include raccoons, foxes (*Urocyon cinereoargenteus*), opossums (*Didelphis virginiana*), skunks (*Mephitis mephitis*), and crows (*Corvus brachyrhynchos*) (Mitchell and Klemens 2000). The introduced house cat (free-ranging and feral [*Felis silvestris*]) is also included in this category because they kill large numbers of native animals (Mitchell and Beck 1992). Populations of raccoons and other subsidized predators, especially cats, are likely contributing to declines in some native species populations at BOWA. An evaluation of the size of the feral cat and raccoon populations in the park, as well as mapping their distribution in relation to park use activities, should be undertaken. Identification of primary turtle nesting sites and evaluation of nest loss to raccoons and other subsidized predators should also be conducted. Such information would allow informed management decisions about control of the cat and raccoon populations.

Captive-raised or captive-bred amphibians and reptiles should not be released at BOWA under any circumstances. It is against Virginia Department of Game and Inland Fisheries law for any species to be released after being held in captivity. The potential for disease introduction is growing and every effort should be made to avoid contamination from exotics or native species from other areas. Captivity often induces stress and influences development of disease. The public should not be allowed to release any animals that have been in captivity and park management should educate park visitors on this issue.

Literature Cited

Blomberg, S., and R. Shine. 1996. Reptiles. Pages 218–226 *in* W. J. Sutherland, editor. Ecological Census Techniques, a Handbook. Cambridge University Press. Cambridge, UK.

Braswell, A. L. 1988. Preliminary report on a survey of the herpetofauna of Cape Hatteras National Seashore. Unpublished report submitted to the National Park Service. NC State Museum of Natural Sciences. Raleigh, NC. 13 pp.

Brown, J. D., J. M. Richards, J. Robertson, S. Holladay, and J. M. Sleeman. 2004. Pathology of aural abscesses in free-living box turtles (*Terrapene carolina carolina*). Journal of Wildlife Diseases 40:704–712.

Buhlmann, K. A. 2001. Terrestrial habitat use by aquatic turtles from a seasonally fluctuating wetland: implications for wetland conservation boundaries. Chelonian Conservation and Biology 4:115-127.

Carter, S. L., C. A. Haas, and J. C. Mitchell. 1999. Home range and habitat selection of bog turtles in southwestern Virginia. Journal of Wildlife Management 63:853–860.

Conant, R., and J. T. Collins. 1998. A Field Guide to Reptiles and Amphibians Eastern and Central North America. 3rd expanded edition. Peterson Field Guide Series. Houghton Mifflin Co. Boston, MA. 616 pp.

Corn, P. S., and R. B. Bury. 1990. Sampling methods for terrestrial amphibians and reptiles. U.S. Department of Agriculture, Forest Service. General Technical Report PNW-GTR-256.

Crother, B. I. (committee chair). 2000. Scientific and standard English names of amphibians and reptiles of North America north of Mexico, with comments regarding confidence in our understanding. SSAR Herpetological Circular 29:1–82.

Dodd, C. K., Jr. 2001. North American Box Turtles, A Natural History. University of Oklahoma Press. Norman, OK. 231 pp.

Forester, D. C. 2000. Amphibian inventory Chesapeake and Ohio Canal and National Historic Park. Unpublished report to the National Park Service. Washington, DC. 62 pp.

Garber, S. D., and J. Burger. 1995. A 20-year study documenting the relationship between turtle decline and human recreation. Ecological Applications 5:1151–1162.

Gibbons, J. W., and R. D. Semlitsch. 1981. Terrestrial drift fences with pitfall traps: an effective technique for quantitative sampling of animal populations. Brimleyana 7:1–16.

Gibbons, J. W., and R. D. Semlitsch. 1987. Activity patterns. Pp. 396–421 *in* R. A. Seigel, J. T. Collins, and S. S. Novak, editors. Snakes: Ecology and Evolutionary Biology. Macmillan Publishing Co. New York, NY.

Gibbons, J. W., V. J. Burke, J. E. Lovich, R. D. Semlitsch, T. D. Tuberville, J. R. Bodie, J. R. Greene, P. H. Niewiarowski, H. H. Whiteman, D. E. Scott, and others. 1997. Perceptions of species abundance, distribution, and diversity: lessons from four decades of sampling on a government-managed reserve. Environmental Management 21:259–268.

Gregory, P. T., J. M. Macartney, and K. W. Larsen. 1987. Spatial patterns and movements. Pages 366–395 *in* R. A. Seigel, J. T. Collins, and S. S. Novak, editors. Snakes: Ecology and Evolutionary Biology. Macmillan Publishing Co. New York, NY.

Heyer, W. R., M. A. Donnelly, R. W. McDiarmid, L. C. Hayek, and M. S. Foster. 1994. Measuring and Monitoring Biological Diversity, Standard Methods for Amphibians. Smithsonian Institution Press. Washington, DC. 364 pp.

Hobson, C. S. 1997. A natural heritage inventory of groundwater invertebrates within the Virginia portions of the George Washington Memorial Parkway including Great Falls Park. Natural Heritage Technical Report 97-9. Virginia Department of Conservation and Recreation, Division of Natural Heritage. Richmond. Unpublished report submitted to the National Park Service. 36 pp. + appendix.

Hobson, C. S. 1998. A natural heritage inventory of the Cheatham and Wormley Pond drainages, Colonial National Historical Park. Natural Heritage Technical Report 98-11. Virginia Department of Conservation and Recreation, Division of Natural Heritage. Richmond, VA. 42 pp. + appendices.

Holladay, S. D., J. C. Wolf, S. A. Smith, D. E. Jones, and J. L. Robertson. 2001. Aural abscesses in wild-caught box turtles (*Terrapene carolina*): possible role of organochlorine-induced hypervitaminosis A. Ecotoxicology and Environmental Safety 48:99–106.

Jones, K. B. 1986. Amphibians and reptiles. Pages 267–290 *in* A. Y. Cooperrider, R. J. Boyd, and H. R. Stuart, editors. Inventory and Monitoring of Wildlife Habitat. U.S. Dept. of Interior, Bureau of Land Management Service Center. Denver, CO.

Leiden, Y. A., M. E. Dorcas, and J. W. Gibbons. 1999. Herpetofaunal diversity in Coastal Plain communities of South Carolina. Journal of the Elisha Mitchell Scientific Society 115:270–280.

Martof, B. S., W. M. Palmer, J. R. Bailey, and J. R. Harrison, III. 1980. Amphibians and Reptiles of the Carolinas and Virginia. University of North Carolina Press. Chapel Hill, NC. 264 pp.

McDiarmid, R. W., and J. C. Mitchell. 2000. Diversity and distribution of amphibians and reptiles. Pages 15–69 *in* D. W. Sparling, G. Linder, and C. A. Bishop (eds.).

Ecotoxicology of Amphibians and Reptiles. Society of Environmental Toxicology and Chemistry, SETAC Press. Pensacola, FL.

Mitchell, J. C. 1994. The Reptiles of Virginia. Smithsonian Institution Press. Washington, DC. 352 pp.

Mitchell, J. C. 2000a. Amphibian Monitoring Methods & Field Guide. Smithsonian National Zoological Park, Conservation Research Center. Front Royal, VA. 56 pp.

Mitchell, J. C. 2000b. Amphibians and reptiles of the National Capital Parks: Review of existing information and inventory methods. Unpublished report to the National Park Service. Washington, DC. 50 pp.

Mitchell, J. C., and J. M. Anderson. 1994. Amphibians and Reptiles of Assateague and Chincoteague Islands. Virginia Museum of Natural History. Martinsville, VA. 120 pp.

Mitchell, J. C., and R. A. Beck. 1992. Free-ranging domestic cat predation on native vertebrates in rural and urban Virginia. Virginia Journal of Science 43:197–207.

Mitchell, J. C., and M. W. Klemens. 2000. Primary and secondary effects of habitat alteration. Pages 5–32 in M. W. Klemens, editor. Turtle Conservation. Smithsonian Institution Press. Washington, DC.

Mitchell, J. C., and K. K. Reay. 1999. Atlas of Amphibians and Reptiles in Virginia. Special Publication Number 1. Virginia Department of Game and Inland Fisheries. Richmond, VA. 122 pp.

Pauley, T. K., J. C. Mitchell, R. R. Buech, and J. J. Moriarty. 2000. Ecology and management of riparian habitats for amphibians and reptiles. Pp. 169–192 in E. S. Verry, J. W. Hornbeck, and C. A. Dolloff (eds.). Riparian Management in Forests of the Continental Eastern United States. Lewis Publishers. Boca Raton, FL.

Radford, A. E., H. E. Ahles, and C. R. Bell. 1968. Manual of the Vascular Flora of the Carolinas. University of North Carolina Press. Chapel Hill, NC. 1,183 pp.

Reinert, H. K. 1993. Habitat selection in snakes. Pages 201–240 in R. A. Seigel and J.T. Collins (eds.), Snakes: Ecology and Behavior. McGraw Hill, Inc. New York, NY.

Relyea, R. A. 2004. Growth and survival of five amphibian species exposed to combinations of pesticides. Environmental Toxicology and Chemistry 23:1737–1742.

Relyea, R. A., and N. Mills. 2001. Predator-induced stress makes the pesticide carbaryl more deadly to gray treefrog tadpoles (Hyla versicolor). Proceeding of the National Academy of Science 98:2491–2496.

Relyea, R. A. 2005. The lethal impact of Roundup on aquatic and terrestrial amphibians. Ecological Applications 15:1118–1124.

Ryan, T. J., T. Philippi, Y. A. Leiden, M. E. Dorcas, T. B. Wigley, and J. W. Gibbons. 2002. Monitoring herpetofauna in a managed forest landscape: effects of habitat types and census techniques. Forest Ecology and Management 167:83–90.

Semlitsch, R. D. 1998. Biological delineation of terrestrial buffer zones for pond-breeding salamanders. Conservation Biology 12:1113–1119.

Semlitsch, R. D. 2003. Conservation of pond-breeding amphibians. Pages. 8–23 *in* R. D. Semlitsch, editor. Amphibian Conservation. Smithsonian Institution Press. Washington, DC.

Semlitsch, R. D., and J. R. Bodie. 1998. Are small, isolated wetlands expendable? Conservation Biology 12:1129–1133.

Semlitsch, R. D., and J. B. Jensen. 2001. Core habitat, not buffer zone. National Wetlands Newsletter 23(4):5–6, 11.

Tuberville, T. D., J. D. Williams, M. E. Dorcas, and J. W. Gibbons. 2005. Herpetofaunal species richness of southeastern national parks. Southeastern Naturalist 4(3):537–569.

Whiteman, H. H., T. M. Mills, D. E. Scott, and J. W. Gibbons. 1995. Confirmation of a range extension for the pine woods snake (*Rhadinaea flavilata*). Herpetological Review 26:158.

Wright, A. H., and A. A. Wright. 1957. Handbook of Snakes of the United States and Canada. 2 Vols. Cornell University Press. Ithaca, NY. 1105 pp.

Appendix A. Checklist of potential of amphibian and reptile species at Booker T. Washington National Monument. The checklist is based on known distributions of amphibians and reptiles in Virginia. The species actually occurring on BOWA is a subset of this list.

CLASS AMPHIBIA

Order Anura	**Frogs and Toads**
Family Bufonidae	Toads
Bufo americanus americanus Holbrook	eastern American toad
Bufo fowleri Hinckley	Fowler's toad
Family Hylidae	Treefrogs
Acris crepitans crepitans Baird	eastern cricket frog
Hyla chrysoscelis Cope	Cope's gray treefrog
Hyla versicolor LeConte	eastern gray treefrog
Pseudacris crucifer crucifer Wied-Neuwied	northern spring peeper
Pseudacris feriarum feriarum (Baird)	upland chorus frog
Family Ranidae	True Frogs
Rana catesbeiana Shaw	American bullfrog
Rana clamitans melanota (Rafinesque)	northern green frog
Rana palustris LeConte	pickerel frog
Order Caudata	**Salamanders**
Family Ambystomatidae	Mole Salamanders
Ambystoma maculatum (Shaw)	spotted salamander
Ambystoma opacum (Gravenhorst)	marbled salamander
Family Plethodontidae	Lungless Salamanders
Desmognathus fuscus (Green)	northern dusky salamander
Desmognathus monticola Dunn	seal salamander
Eurycea cirrigera (Green)	northern two-lined salamander
Eurycea guttolineata (Holbrook)	three-lined salamander
Gyrinophilus porphyriticus porphyriticus (Green)	northern spring salamander
Hemidacty lium scutatum (Schlegel)	four-toed salamander
Plethodon cinereus (Green)	red-backed salamander
Plethodon cylindraceus (Harlan)	white-spotted slimy salamander
Pseudotriton ruber ruber (Latreille)	northern red salamander
Family Salamandridae	True Salamanders
Notophthalmus viridescens viridescens (Rafinesque)	red-spotted newt
CLASS REPTILIA	
Order Testudines	**Turtles**
Family Chelydridae	Snapping Turtles
Chelydra serpentina serpentina (Linnaeus)	eastern snapping turtle
Family Emydidae	Pond Turtles
Chrysemys picta picta (Schneider)	eastern painted turtle
Terrapene carolina carolina (Linnaeus)	eastern box turtle
Family Kinosternidae	Mud and Musk Turtles
Sternotherus odoratus (Latreille)	eastern musk turtle
Order Squamata	**Lizards, Snakes, and Amphisbaenians**
Suborder Sauria	**Lizards**
Family Phrynosomatidae	Sceloporine Lizards
Sceloporus undulatus hyacinthinus (Green)	northern fence lizard
Family Scincidae	Skinks
Eumeces fasciatus (Linnaeus)	five-lined skink
Eumeces laticeps (Schneider)	broad-headed skink
Scincella lateralis (Say)	little brown skink
Family Teiidae	Tegus and Whiptails
Cnemidophorus sexlineatus sexlineatus (Linnaeus)	eastern six-lined racerunner

Appendix A. Checklist of potential of amphibian and reptile species at Booker T. Washington National Monument. The checklist is based on known distributions of amphibians and reptiles in Virginia. The species actually occurring on BOWA is a subset of this list (continued).

CLASS AMPHIBIA	
Order Squamata	**Lizards, Snakes, and Amphisbaenians**
Suborder Serpentes	**Snakes**
Family Colubridae	Colubrids
Carphophis amoenus amoenus (Say)	eastern wormsnake
Coluber constrictor constrictor Linnaeus	northern black racer
Diadophis punctatus edwardsii (Merrem)	northern ring-necked snake
Elaphe obsoleta obsoleta (Say)	eastern ratsnake
Heterodon platirhinos Latreille	eastern hog-nosed snake
Lampropeltis calligaster rhombomaculata (Holbrook)	mole kingsnake
Lampropeltis getula getula (Linnaeus)	eastern kingsnake
Nerodia sipedon sipedon (Linnaeus)	northern watersnake
Opheodrys aestivus (Linnaeus)	rough greensnake
Regina septemvittata (Say)	queen snake
Storeria dekayi dekayi (Holbrook)	northern brownsnake
Storeria occipitomaculata occipitomaculata (Storer)	northern red-bellied snake
Thamnophis sauritus sauritus (Linnaeus)	eastern ribbonsnake
Thamnophis sirtalis sirtalis (Linnaeus)	eastern gartersnake
Family Viperidae	Vipers and Pitvipers
Agkistrodon contortrix mokasen (Palisot de Beauvois)	northern copperhead

* Observed by Joe Mitchell and field crew 2003 -2004

Appendix B. Amphibian and reptile survey dates and sampling methods at Booker T. Washington National Monument during May 9 2002 and in 2003 and 2004.

Method	Dates of field trips
VES	2002: May 9; 2003: Mar. 21, May 14, Jun. 2–3, Jul. 9, Sep. 27; 2004: May 29
Dipnets	2003: Mar. 20
Minnow traps	2003: None
Turtle traps	2003: None
Road Survey	2003: None
Audio	2003: Mar. 20–21, May 14

Appendix C. List of photographic images of amphibians and reptiles for Booker T. Washington National Monument. All images (jpg files) are coded by BOWA-Number and Scientific name (e.g., BOWA-1 B. *americanus*).

Image #	Scientific name	Common name	Notes
	Frogs		
BOWA-1	*Bufo americanus*	American toad	BOWA specimen
BOWA-2	*Hyla chrysoscelis*	Cope's gray treefrog	BOWA specimen
BOWA-3	*Pseudacris crucifer*	northern spring peeper	from APCO
BOWA-4	*Rana catesbeiana*	American bullfrog	BOWA specimen
BOWA-5	*Rana clamitans*	northern green frog	from APCO
	Salamanders		
BOWA-6	*Desmognathus fuscus*	northern dusky salamander	BOWA specimen
BOWA-7	*Eurycea cirrigera*	southern two-lined salamander	BOWA specimen
BOWA-8	*Gyrinophilus porphyriticus*	northern spring salamander	BOWA specimen
BOWA-9	*Pseudotriton ruber*	northern red salamander	from RICH
	Turtles		
BOWA-10	*Chelydra serpentina*	snapping turtle	BOWA specimen
BOWA-11	*Terrapene carolina*	eastern box turtle	BOWA specimen
	Lizards		
BOWA-12	*Eumeces fasciatus*	five-lined skink	BOWA specimen
BOWA-13	*Sceloporus undulatus*	northern fence lizard	BOWA specimen
	Snakes		
BOWA-14	*Carphophis amoenus*	eastern worm snake	BOWA specimen
BOWA-15	*Diadophis punctatus*	northern ring-necked snake	BOWA specimen
BOWA-16	*Elaphe obsoleta*	black ratsnake	BOWA specimen; 2 images
BOWA-17	*Nerodia sipedon*	northern watersnake	BOWA specimen; 2 images
BOWA-18	*Storeria occipitomaculata*	red-bellied snake	from PETE

NPS D-037 September 2006